D1646090

Málaga

The Capital of the Sun Coast

Contents

Excursions

Worth Knowing

Some historical facts

▶ **How Málaga changed during the centuries**

From the estate to the provincial capital

Málaga was founded around 770 BC by Phoenician sailors setting up a settlement next to the hill the Alcazaba is located on, who named the city "Malaka", which derives from "malak" (salting the fish).

The Phoenicians succeeded the Greeks and 206 CE onwards the city became part of the Roman Empire.

In the days of migration and the decline of the Roman Empire in the 6th century, Málaga suffered from numerous invasions by Germanic tribes.

Stability brought the reign of the Byzantine empire, which ended with the invasion of the Moors in 711 CE. After that Málaga became an important business centre.

Several buildings were constructed, culture and science began to flourish. Between 1237 and 1487 the port was the most significant connection to North Africa for the Nasrid Dynasty reigning in Granada.

The second great heyday of the city started after its conquest on the 18th of August in 1487 by the Catholic Monarchs in the course of the Reconquest.

Numerous changes in structure and urban development turned Málaga into a new Christian settlement.

The 16th and 17th centuries were marked by epidemics, floods and crop failures but from the 18th century onwards, the city began to recover.

A modern port was constructed and repair works at the cathedral came to an end.

Due to the industrialisation in the 19th century the cityscape continued to change. The upper classes arose, which were maintained by the families Larios and Heredia. The streets Marqués de Larios and Alameda were introduced in their name.

During the Spanish Civil War, Málaga was located near the front and served as a port for the republican Spanish marine. As the rebel faction commanded by Franco managed to approach the city with the help of Italian soldiers, 150,000 inhabitants were forced to flee towards Almeria on the 8th of February in 1937. They were bombed and shelled by warships. Up to 10,000 people died in the massacre of Málaga.

Under the dictatorship of Franco, tourism on the Costa del Sol began to boom and Málaga became a modern European capital whose daily life was enriched by a diverse mixture of culture. Málaga is the second most populous city of Andalusia (after Seville) with approximately 570,000 inhabitants and is the sixth largest city in Spain.

Málaga today

Pablo Picasso's hometown is characterised by a long history influenced by different cultures and nations. It is one of the oldest cities in the world.

It is these influences and the benign climate with around 300 sunny days in a year and a short, mild winter that make this city so attractive. Those who are interested in relaxing from the sights will be impressed by a landscape rich in contrast.

On the outskirts, Málaga is surrounded by fertile land and the protecting heights of Sierra de Mijas as well as by the Montes de Málaga, which are up to 2,000 metres high. Furthermore, Málaga's beaches extend almost 14 kilometres, are 25 metres wide and beautiful seaside promenades line the city.

Several parks, gardens and avenues invite visitors to go for a stroll. Tapas bars, bodegas and elegant restaurants promise culinary delights on a high level. The streets pulsate with life and numerous boutiques and shops in the pedestrian zone tempt the visitor with great offers. Málaga has become a cultural metropolis for tourists and students due to sheer creativeness and commitment.

But in spite of all the innovations, the inhabitants of Málaga still know how to preserve their traditions and Andalusian aura.

A Walk through the city

▶ **Explore the birthplace of Picasso**

Tracing the roots of Picasso

A walk through the hometown of Picasso begins at the Plaza del Obispo in front of the ① Bishop's Palace (18th century), which impresses with its baroque façade and the magnificent main portal of the ② Cathedral La Encarnación, one of the most splendid Renaissance churches measuring almost 48 metres in height, 72 metres in width and 119 metres in length. Following the wrought-iron grid, the Calle de Santa Maria is right ahead, allowing visitors to enter the cathedral via a side entrance, which is bordered by orange trees and limited by a small garden. Afterwards the walk will lead to one of the picturesque little streets in the old town, the Calle San Agustín.

Bishop's Palace

The Convento de San Agustín Church (16th century) is located here and consists of the church, a college and a residence for the monks. The courtyard adjacent to the ③ Museo Picasso Málaga is located inside the Palace of Count Buenavista.

Tip: Every Sunday, entry is free during the last two hours.

Turn right at the end of the street to reach the Calle Granada and the ④ Church of Santiago Apóstol (15th-18th centuries), the oldest church in Málaga, in which Picasso was baptised on the 10th of November in 1881 - indicated by the front of the church.

Furthermore, to the left, the Antigua Farmacia Mamely (1739) can be seen, which has an information board mentioning the Picasso family.

Cathedral La Encarnación

Buenavista Palace

Mercy Square

In the 19th century, the architect Rafael Mitjana erected a statue on Málaga's oldest and most famous square to the General Don José Maria Torrijos and his 48 comrades who were put before a firing squad at Málaga's beach in 1831. The obelisk, decorated with a laurel wreath made up of 49 crowns, rises up in the sky, thus honouring each soldier killed. In the plinth of the monument, a crypt is built in with the mortal remains of the freedom fighters and the two basic principles of the city, namely "Liberty and Justice".

Visitors will come across the bronze statue of Pablo Picasso sitting on a bench, designed by Francisco L. Hernandez. Supposedly, Picasso's famous picture of the white dove was taken here.

Mercy Square

House number 15, in which Picasso was born on the 25th of October in 1881, is located just behind and is nowadays known as the ⑤ Museo Casa Natal de Picasso. It houses important lithographs and documents of the artist, while in a second building the Picasso Foundation exhibits Picasso's works, which he produced during his stay in Paris.

Tip: You can buy a combined ticket for both buildings.

twitter.com /laplazamm

Those interested in visiting the Cervantes Theatre (19th century) need to pass the Calle San Juan de Letran, which leads to the forecourt of the theatre. The Cervantes Theatre is counted among the oldest theatres in Europe in its original condition, with a rectangular floor plan and ceiling frescos by Bernado Ferrándiz illustrating industry, business and the port.

Picasso in front of his birthplace   *Showroom of the Picasso foundation*

By going round the square along tapas bars the Calle Alcazabilla can be reached, which runs parallel to the Calle Granada. The Roman Theatre is located next to the Alcazaba and dates back to Emperor Augustus' time (1st century BC) although it was not detected before 1951 during construction works. Nowadays, it is used for classic plays, concerts and dances.

Just behind, the ⑥ Alcazaba rears up on a hill. This fortress was constructed by the Moorish Sultan Badis and was later on expanded by the Nasrids into a palace (11th-14th centuries).

The footpath to the Castillo de Gibralfaro (Paseo Don Juan Temboury) lies between the entrance and the Aduana Palace.

Tip: You can buy a combined ticket for both attractions. Entry is free on Sundays from 2pm onwards.

Plaza del General Torrijos

The following street Travesia Pintor Nogales leads to the ⑦ Casa del Jardinero, the gardener's house (1908), which is surrounded by rich vegetation and served as accommodation for the head gardener of the municipality. Turn left to reach the Avenida de Cervantes.

The former Post Office and Telegraph Building in neo-mudejar style was inaugurated in 1923 and used as such until 1986. Nowadays, the ⑧ Rectory and the Administration of the University of Málaga are located in this oriental building.

The two big locations headed by the University of Málaga are the campus El Ejido and the campus Teatinos, with approximately 40,000 students.

Rectory of the University of Málaga

Following the model of a Greco-Roman temple, the architect José Yarnoz constructed the building of the ⑨ Bank of Spain in the neo-classicist style (20th century).

The ⑩ City Council (20th century) is based next to the Bank of Spain and counts among the monuments of the city due to its magnificent façade in the neo-baroque style. The Plenary Hall and the Hall of Mirrors exhibit important oil paintings.

The walk continues through the gardens laid out by Pedro Luis Alonso. Mediterranean orange trees and a variety of 75 roses lend a specific flair to the small park.

At the level of the decorative pools, cross Málaga's boulevard Paseo de Parque to the right and stroll left along the shady tropical and subtropical plants.

Bank of Spain and City Hall *Gardens of Pedro Luis Alonso*

The view falls on the ⑪ Plaza del General Torrijos, the Hospital Noble (19th century) in a neo-gothic style and the ⑫ bullring "La Malagueta" (1874) constructed by Joaquín Rucoba in the neo-mudejar style and ranking nowadays amongst the oldest and most beautiful bullrings in Spain.

The circular building is 50 metres in diameter and consists of approximately 14,000 seats, four bull enclosures, ten pastures, stud farms and an infirmary. A museum houses exhibits from more than six centuries of tauromachy.

After crossing the Avenida Cánovas del Castillo, the Paseo de la Farola can be reached, leading to the ⑬ lighthouse "La Farola" (1816). The famous section of the beach "La Malagueta" is right in front of "La Farola".

Playa de la Malagueta

Heading back to the seaside promenade (Muello Uno), visitors will come across expensive yachts, elegant restaurants and boutiques and by the promenade El Palmeral de las Sorpresas (2011) where 408 palms and thousands of bushes and plants are growing.

After a short walk, visitors will get to the ⑭ Plaza de la Marina connecting the port with the historical centre where the Port Work Committee (1935) is located as well as the Sculpture of Cenachero (1964) constructed by Jaime Fernandez Pimentel and provided with a dedication to the poet Salvador Rueda.

At the information centre of the tourist department, visitors will cross the Plaza de la Marina and Málaga's avenue Alameda Principal, where the Culture Department can be found.

Seaside promenade

Cenachero

The bronze statue of Hans Christian Andersen, a work by José María Córdoba, which was erected on the occasion of the author's 200th birthday, stands on the right side.

Since 1899, year of the construction of the monument, Manuel Domingo Larios y Larios' view has been falling on the street of the same name (Calle Marqués de Larios), which is regarded as the city's main shopping district and scene of the famous Feria.

The history of this notorious street dates back to 1880 as the citizens voted for the construction of a central street instead of investing the money in the extension of the cathedral's second tower — nowadays called lovingly "La Manquita — the One-Armed" as part of a referendum on the use of funds.

Hustle and bustle on the Alameda Principal

As part of a stroll on the Calle Marqués de Larios to ⑮ Plaza de la Constitución (Square of the Constitution), visitors pass by elegant boutiques and the sculpture "Points of View" by the British sculptor Tony Cragg.

After the conquest by the Christians, the Plaza became the city's centre and was called Plaza Mayor (Main Plaza) or Plaza de las Cuatro Calles (Plaza of the Four Streets). In 1812 it received its current name.

Until 1869, the City Council was located here. Numerous beautiful municipal halls are situated around the plaza, such as the old Jesuit college San Telmo and the Casa del Consulado, which remind visitors of by-gone eras.

The marble Source of Genoa (16th century) is said to originate in Genoa. This Source was created by an

Plaza de la Constitución

unknown artist in the Renaissance style and consists of an dodecagonal basin, the fronts of which are decorated with Ionic themes.

In December 1978, the democratic constitution came into force after the dictatorship of Franco had fallen.

The covers of famous Spanish newspapers reporting on this historical event are embedded in the plaza's ground as metal plates. Nowadays, this place is considered famous for several events and concerts.

Beautiful restaurants are located in the Pasaje de Chinitas, where tasty tapas can be enjoyed.

The Calle de Santa Maria next to the Café Central, in which several souvenir shops follow one another, leads back to the Cathedral.

Lunch in the Historical Centre

Churches and Chapels

Worth seeing

Cathedral La Encarnación

This Cathedral is said to be one of the most splendid Renaissance churches in Andalusia. Emperor Charles V. began to construct the Cathedral in 1528 on the floor plan of the central mosque, but in 1782 the construction was irrevocably stopped.

Owing to a construction time of nearly 254 years, the Cathedral unites several architectural styles, amongst them late Gothic, Renaissance and Baroque.

The interior, which will impress with its size, has three naves while the ceiling is made of open vaults with 23 byzantine cupolas on 46 pillars. The side aisles, as well as the ambulatory, contain 15 chapels and 25 altars of unimaginable value with paintings and statues partly dating back to their formation.

The choir has 42 high reliefs carved by Pedro de Mena, whose holy statues are characterised by great vivacity, flanked by two organs (1779 and 1781) with more than 4,000 pipes.

The Madonna of Nuestra Señora de los Reyes, which can be admired in a chapel located next to the Ambulatory, was created by a Castilian artist in the 14th century.

It is also worth seeing the Capilla Rosario, which is dominated by Alonso Cano's rosary Madonna.

The Cathedral received its first two bells in 1785, named La Encarnación (1.93m in diameter, 4,162 kg) and La Concepción (1.81m in diameter, 3,433 kg), which have, up to now, been recognised as the biggest and heaviest bells in the world. The chiming later on expanded with twelve bells and a carillon.

More art treasures can be admired in the Cathedral's museum in the rooms of the former chapter house.

Visitors will be able to visit the roof of the Cathedral and admire the panoramic views. For further information contact bovedas.catedral@diocesismalaga.es or go along to the Palacio Episcopal.

Address: Calle Molina Lario, 9

diocesismalaga.es/catedral

Garden of the Cathedral

Santa Ana Abbey

The Cistercian Abbey was built in 1878 by Jerónimo Cuervo and was restored in 1990.

The temple consists of a nave divided into three parts and roofed with a barrel vault.

The main chapel has the form of a semicircle and has a cupola. Typical examples of sacred convent art are the choir and the tribune located behind the chancel. The portal, made of white stones, consists of a circular arch with salient Tuscan pilasters.

The statue of Santa Ana (18th century) in terracotta is nestled in the façade.

Address: Calle Cister, 13

malagaturismo.com

Santa Ana Abbey

Basílica of Santa María de la Victoria TIP

The basilica was originally planned as a pilgrimage church (15th century) and is dedicated to the Virgen de la Victoria, the Patron of Málaga. Due to dilapidation, a new building with a tower-shrine in baroque style was erected around 1700. The church consists of a Latin-Cross design.

The crypt of the Counts of Buenavista with white stucco on black background and the Shrine of Our Lady of Victoria in baroque and rococo style are both worth seeing.

Address: Plaza del Santuario

malagaturismo.com

Basílica of Santa María de la Victoria

Del Agua Chapel

This chapel of processional origin in baroque style was built around 1800 into the front of the house. The façade embodies a large arch. The polygonal interior is covered with hemispherical domes decorated with stucco ornaments.

The images of Cristo del Rescate and de la Virgen de Gracia used in processions can be admired here.

Address: Calle Agua, 1

malagaturismo.com

Del Agua Chapel

San Lázaro Chapel

The Chapel, in Mudejar style, was founded in 1491 by the Catholic Monarchs originally as part of the San Lázaro hospital for lepers. Nowadays, only the chapel is preserved. Since 1711, it has been the seat of two fraternities.

The nave with its chancel is covered with two wooden roof trusses, of which the one in the nave is square and the one in the chancel is rectangular.

It is worth mentioning the picture of Saint Joseph of the 17th century. The respective fraternities' pictures of the saints are not only fixed on the neo-baroque retable but also on the side altar.

Address: Plaza de la Victoria, 19

malagaturismo.com

San Lázaro Chapel

Convento de San Agustín Church

Thanks to the particular meaning of doctrine for the Order of Saint Augustine, the convent has three parts: a church, school and the monks' residence.

It was founded in the 16th century but today's church dates from the 18th century.

The church consists of three naves. The main nave is roofed with a barrel vault and surrounded with transverse arches and lunettes. The barrel vaults at the roof are crowned with beams decorated with a line of oval forms and pearls.

Address: Calle San Agustín, 7

agustinosescorial.com

Convento de San Agustín Church

Santos Mártires Church

Erected in the 15th century in Mudejar style this church is regarded as one of the most beautiful examples of rococo architecture after having undergone many renovations. It consists of three naves and the interior impresses with rich Baroque decorations. A huge coat of arms rises above the altar.

The church was founded in 1494 in honour of the saints San Ciriacio and Santa Paula, and is Málaga's only place of worship that incorporates five canonical brotherhoods.

Address: Plaza de los Mártires, 1

santosmartires.es

Santos Mártires Church

Sagrario Church

This small church is built on the floor plan of the main mosque, as is the Cathedral. It once served the Moors as an entrance hall to the mosque.

It was not until 1498 that the striking portal in Elizabethan gothic style was created as the entrance to the Cathedral. Later on, the sides were closed and the entrance hall eventually became a church.

The interior, in baroque style dating from the 18th century, consists of a nave and a choir with an altarpiece in plateresque style.

Address: Calle Santa María, 22

malaga.us/top-attractions.htm

Saint John The Baptist Church

The construction of this parish church began in 1487 as the Catholic Monarchs had conquered the city, after which it was divided into four parishes, namely San Juan, Santiago, Mártires and Sagrario.

Today's appearance of this church as well as the inscriptions on the façade dates from the 18th century when the ruined tower was replaced by a tower with a colonnade.

Address: Calle San Juan, 3

malagaturismo.com

Santo Cristo de la Salud Church

After the Jesuits had carried out missionary work in Málaga, they founded the church named "Santo Cristo" in the 16th century, as the small pilgrimage church Ermita de San Sebastían did not satisfy their needs.

The interior, dating from the 17th century, impresses with an overwhelming altar that consists of an ornate shrine, in which the consecrated hosts are kept. The murals in the cupola were only completed in 1643.

Address: Calle Compañía, 4
santocristomalaga.blogspot.de

Santo Cristo de la Salud Church

San Felipe de Neri Church

The church is also known as Santa Cruz, and is located in the district of San Felipe Neri. The construction of this church stems back to a chapel that the Count of Buenavista built between 1720 and 1730 next to his city palace.

The classical façade is equipped with a portal in two doors situated between two towers. The side portals are decorated with solid curved elements. The exterior wall of the former chapel is topped with intertwined geometric forms in ochre and red. It is worth seeing the 18th century's wood carvings in the interior of the church.

Address: Calle Cabello, 20
malagaturismo.com

San Felipe de Neri Church

Santiago Church

This church was erected in 1490 after the Reconquest on the site of a former mosque and nowadays counts among one of Málaga's oldest churches. Of the original façade, only the central entrance in the Mudejar style remained. The former separate minaret became the church tower in the 16th century. In one of the left-hand-side nave's chapels, the statue of Jesus The Rich, a valuable cross made of wood and silver, is located in the baroque interior. Pablo Picasso was baptised in this church on the 10th of November in 1881. His certificate of baptism is exhibited here.

Address: Calle Granada, 78

parroquiasantiago.es

Santiago Church

La Ermita Zamarrilla

The foundations for this small chapel at the border of the districts El Perchel and La Trinidad were laid in 1757. Between 1945 and 1999 the chapel was restored.

It owes its name to the famous legend of a bandit named Zamarrilla who was looking for refuge under the statue of the Virgin Mary.

As soon as the danger had passed, he took a knife and stabbed himself in the chest in pure admiration of the Virgin Mary.

Address: Calle Martínez Maldonado, 5

zamarrilla.es

La Ermita Zamarrilla

Monuments and Palaces

Discover all the great things to visit

Alcazaba

The Alcazaba was built in the 11ᵗʰ century by the Moor sultan Badis and served not only as a palace but also as a fortress. It is divided into two paved parts, the outer citadel of which was part of the defence system that used to be connected with the city wall but nowadays is dismantled.

The vault gate leads to the first area, once used as the chapel and armoury. A labyrinth of corridors and arches alternates with ornately laid-out gardens and fountains.

The inner citadel consists of the palace, made up of three courts. The impressive colonnade in the caliph style offers amazing views of the city.

Nowadays, some of the rooms are used for particular exhibitions and the Archaeological Museum exhibits prehistoric finds relevant to the city's history and the famous green ceramics of Málaga (12ᵗʰ-14ᵗʰ centuries).

Address: Calle Alcazabilla

andalucia.com/cities/malaga/alcazaba.htm

malaga.us/top-attractions.htm

Tip: You can buy a combined ticket with Gibralfaro. Entry is free on Sundays from 2pm onwards.

Roman Theatre

The Roman Theatre is located at the Alcazaba's Western slope. It dates from the times of Emperor Augustus (1st century BC) and was only detected in 1951 during construction works. The auditorium is over 31 metres wide and more than 16 metres tall. The rows of seats are constructed on a slope.

Until the 3rd century AD it served as a theatre for the Romans. After the Moors had reconquered the city, they used the quarry for new buildings and over the course of time it disappeared under coats of soil.

Nowadays, classical plays, dance performances and concerts take place here.

andalucia.com/cities/malaga/teatro-romano.htm

Tip: Entry is free.

Roman Theatre

Gibralfaro Castle

This Moor castle is located more than 130 metre above sea level and its name can be attributed to a Phoenician lighthouse. The Arabic term Gebel-Faro translates into "rock of the lighthouse".

It was built in 1340 by the caliph Yusuf I and served as a dwelling for the soldiers as well as protection for the Alcazaba, with which it is connected via la Coracha Terrestre, a double laid-out wall-walk.

This enabled the troops to move safely between the castle and the fortress and to repel the enemies on both sides simultaneously.

Along the crenellated walls and towers, it is possible to go round the whole fortress for beautiful views of

Outer citadel

the city, the Mediterranean Sea and the Montes de Málaga. When the weather is clear it is even possible to see the Rif, a mountain chain part of the Atlas Mountains in Morocco and the Strait of Gibraltar.

The old powder magazine exhibits arms, swords and more historically relevant objects.

For those who do not want to go on foot (the path is quite steep) the bus line 35, the tourist bus or the horse and carriage will take you to the castle.

Address: Camino de Gibralfaro, 11

malaga.us/top-attractions.htm

Tip: You can buy a combined ticket with Alcazaba. Entry is free on Sundays from 2pm onwards.

View of the Mediterranean Sea

Episcopal Palace

The Bishop's Palace comprised a whole series of buildings during the 16th to 18th centuries. The late Baroque portal was designed by Antonio Ramos and is characterised by grey marble on pink-coloured pillars. It consists of the entrance, the balcony and the stone statue of the Virgin of Sorrows.

Address: Plaza del Obispo, 6 / Events: arsmalaga.es

Aduana Palace

The Customs Palace (19th century) in the neo-classical style was built on the model of Italian Renaissance palaces. The sturdy stairs have a marble balustrade. The two central entrances lead to the interior.

Address: Plaza Aduana, 1

Aduana Palace

Miramar Palace

The former Hotel Miramar (1926) is a work by the architect Guerrero Strachan and was renovated in 1987 in order to house the Palace of Justice. Now the building is turning into a luxury hotel. The Gran Hotel Miramar will open in late 2016.

Address: Paseo de Reding, 22

granhotelmiramarmalaga.com

Ink Palace

The building has a footprint of about 10,500 square metres and is a work designed by Julio O'Brian in 1908. The headquarters of the Railway Company of Andalusia was located here. The nickname derives from the fact that many employees put "rivers of ink" on paper.

Address: Paseo de Reding, 20

Ink Palace

Buenavista Palace

The Buenavista Palace, a renaissance building dating from the 16th century, was constructed for Diego de Cazalla on the ruins of a Nasrid palace. In the 19th century, this palace became the residence of the Counts of Buenavista, after whom it is named.

It was after the Royal Decree of 1913 when the Museo de Bellas Artes (Museum of Fine Arts) got housed inside the palace, which was declared a National Monument in 1939.

Due to its architectural importance, the Palace was chosen to house the Picasso Museum, which opened its doors in 2003.

Address: Calle San Agustín, 8

Ibn Garbirol Gardens at the rear of the Buenavista Palace

Zea-Salvatierra Palace

The palace was erected in the last years of the 17th century and at the beginning of the 18th century on behalf of María Salvatierra, the widow of Captain Blas de Zea Merino.

On both sides of the two-storey portal, the founders' coat of arms can be seen. There is a series of arches on marble columns made up of Corinthian capitals around the inner courtyard.

During the reign of Isabelle II, this building became Málaga's district council. Afterwards, it served as the main post office until late into the 20th century. Nowadays, this palace is privately owned.

Address: Calle Cister, 1

malagaturismo.com

Zea-Salvatierra Palace

Palacio de Villacázar

This palace was constructed in the 18th century by the Count of Buenavista and is nowadays the Chamber of Commerce. The building has a lookout tower and a passage made of giant marble columns.

Address: Calle Cortina del Muelle, 23

malagaturismo.com

Archivo Municipal

This building of the 18th century houses the Municipal Archive as well as a library. It offers several exhibitions, which are free to visit.

Address: Alameda Principal, 23

archivomunicipal.malaga.eu

Municipal Archive

City Council

TIP

The city hall, built in 1919 by the architects Strachan and Vera, radiates baroque elegance. A broad stairway leads to a portal, over which a balcony is edged with white columns.

The Hall of Mirrors houses oil paintings showing portraits of personalities who are relevant to the city's history. The plenary room shows paintings by Antonio Muñoz Degrain that portray the rescue of the crew of German frigate Gneisenau.

During the Christmas season, the biggest crib (Bélen) of the city is exhibited here with 256 figures in a space over 150 square metres.

Address: Avenida de Cervantes, 4

malaga.eu

City Council

Bank of Spain

The Bank of Spain was built between 1933 and 1936 in neo-classical style by the architect José Yarnoz.

With six Corinthian columns at the main entrance, the building is adapted from a Greco-Roman temple.

Address: Avenida de Cervantes

Rectory of the University of Málaga

The former Post Office building in neo-mudejar style eventually become the Rectory of the University of Málaga in 1986. The Rectory owes its oriental appearance to its square basic form, the main façade with rounded corners and curved towers.

Address: Avenida de Cervantes, 2

Bank of Spain   *Rectory of the University*

Casa del Jardinero

This Gardener's House was built in 1908 as head-quarters for the city's Head Gardener and is located in the midst of a garden, nearly hiding the whole small building.

Address: Avenida de Cervantes, 1

Hospital Noble

The hospital was inaugurated in the 19th century in neo-gothic style on behalf of the testimonial legacy of Dr Joseph Noble, who died in Málaga 1861 during the cholera epidemic and is buried in the city's English Cemetery.

Address: Plaza del General Torrijos, 2

malagaturismo.com

Hospital Noble

Plaza de Toros "La Malagueta"   TIP

This bullring located next to the beach was constructed in 1874 by Joaquín Rucoba in neo-mudejar style.

The arena has 16 sides, is 50 metres in diameter and accommodates around 14,000 spectators. Furthermore, it consists of four bull enclosures, ten pastures, stables, a museum and an aid station. It nowadays still serves as a traditional courtly riding school of the Royal Cavalry of Ronda. During the Holy Week and the August Festival, several bullfighting events take place in this arena when the most famous toreros showcase their talent. Additionally, the bullring is used for concerts, festivals, and cultural/sports events.

Address: Paseo de Reding, 8

entradastorosmalaga.com

Plaza de Toros "La Malagueta"

Atarazanas Central Market

The market was constructed in the 19th century by the architect Joaquín de Rucoba in an iron-trellis construction on the former Moorish shipyard's area. Smaller markets can be found throughout every district.

Address: Calle Atarazanas, 10 / Open: Mon-Sat 8am - 3pm

andalucia.com/cities/malaga/ataranzas-market.htm

Salamanca's Market

The Salamanca's market in neo-Arab style is located in the district of "El Molinillo". It consists of only one nave with two identical opposite entrances. The interior tiles represent fish, birds and fruits.

Address: Calle San Bartolomé, 1

Open: Mon-Sat 8am - 3pm

malagaturismo.com

Atarazanas Central Market   *Salamanca's Market*

Teatro Cervantes

The Teatro Cervantes was constructed in 1870 according to the plans of Jerónimo Cuervo on the vegetable garden of a cathedral and was renovated in the eighties.

Four circles, rising up above the horseshoe-shaped parquet, have room for 1,171 spectators. It is worth seeing the ceiling frescos by Bernado Ferrándiz and the paintings by Muñoz Degrain.

It is Málaga's oldest theatre and besides several cultural events like operas, theatres, dances and music, it is the location of the Spanish Film Festival. At the same time it administrates the reopened Theatre Echegaray and functions as the city's cultural centre.

Address: Calle Ramos Marin, 3

teatrocervantes.com

Teatro Cervantes

Old Warehouses of Félix Sáenz

The former store Félix Sáenz was constructed in 1914 according to Manuel Rivera Vera's plans. This architectural style mixes elements of Mediterranean modernism and neo-baroque. Today the building houses the shop H&M (p. 103).

Address: Plaza Félix Sáenz, 2 / hm.com

Antigua Fábrica de Tabaco

The Old Tobacco Factory, constructed around 1930, consists of three buildings around a large inner court-yard, into which visitors can enter through a marvellous iron gate. Nowadays, the building houses the Automobile Museum and the Russian Art Museum.

Address: Avenida Sor Teresa Prat, 17 / Bus Line 16

Old Tobacco Factory

Consulate House

The Consulate House was built in 1785 as the Agriculturist Relief Fund and later became the headquarters of the Inland and Shipping Consulate. In 1923 it was declared a National Historical Landmark. Currently, the rooms are used by the Economic Society of the Friends of the Country.

Address: Plaza de la Constitución, 7

Atenaeum

Originally, the rooms of the former college of art San Telmo constituted the expansion of the Jesuit Church. Picasso's father used to teach in one of the studios.

Address: Plaza de la Constitución, 3

San Telmo and the Consulate House

City of Museums

Over recent years, Málaga has become a museum city. Currently, more than 30 museums of different topics can be visited, including the Picasso Museum, the exhibition spaces of the Picasso Foundation and Picasso's birthplace. Most of the exhibitions take place in the historical centre and are well connected.

Some of the museums are interactive and promise interesting and informative experiences, not exclusively for families with children. It is notable that most of the exhibits are presented with attention to detail.

Most of the resident fraternities own rooms, in which they exhibit their collections. Some organisations offer thematically-distinct presentations such as the Archaeological Museum in the Alcazaba. Furthermore, several temporary exhibitions can be visited.

It is worth searching for information on special exhibitions on the city's website (www.malagaturismo. com). Tourist offices and the museums' websites also give useful information. Some museums offer free entrance on Sunday afternoons and on the first Sunday of the month.

Centre Pompidou

Located at the port of the city the Centre Pompidou offers temporary exhibitions in a coloured cube.

Address: Pasaje Doctor Carrillo Casaux

centrepompidou-malaga.eu

Centro de Arte Contemporáneo de Málaga (CAC Málaga)   TIP

The Contemporary Art Centre of Málaga is located in a historical building next to riverbed of the Guadelmedina. The collection comprises 400 works from 1950 up to now with special focus being put on works of North-American artists living in the sixties. Furthermore, the centre offers temporary exhibitions of national and international artists, lectures, seminars and workshops. The museum is open to every artistic and cultural characteristic.

Address: Calle Alemania, 2

cacmalaga.eu

Tip: Free to visit

CAC Málaga

Centro de Interpretación del Castillo de Gibralfaro

The Gibralfaro Castle Interpretation Centre was constructed on the grounds of the former gunpowder store. At the gate, visitors can see a large model of the city, its defensive walls during the 16th century, the Castle and the Alcazaba as well as the City Hall, the Cathedral, the Bullring and the Aduana Palace. Large display cases comprising pieces of the 16th to 20th centuries inform visitors about the urban development while weapons, uniforms, and everyday necessities give an impression of the garrison and life on the castle.

Address: Camino de Gibralfaro, 11 / Bus line 35
Tip: On Sundays at 2pm onwards, entry is free.

El Camino de Gibralfaro with observation deck

Fundación Picasso. Museo Casa Natal & Sala de Exposiciones

The Casa Natal Museum and the Museum of the Picasso Foundation exhibit works of art and personal objects of the Picasso family. One office from the 19th century has been duplicated. A specialist library, temporary exhibitions and cultural activities educate visitors about the artist's life and his family. In 1983, this building was declared Historical-Artistic Monument of National Interest.

In another exhibition centre, works of the artist during his residence in Paris are presented.

Address: Plaza de la Merced, 15 & 13

fundacionpicasso.es

Tip: You can buy a combined ticket for both buildings.

Picasso Foundation

MIMMA
Museo Interactivo de la Música

The Interactive Music Museum located in the Palacio del Conde Navas houses the most important collection of Europe with around 1,000 exhibits, 400 of which are part of the permanent exhibition.

Visitors have the chance to experiment with 300 instruments from different epochs, countries and cultures that are exposed in rooms stimulating all senses. Visitors are asked to play these instruments.

Furthermore, the museum has a banquet hall known as the Sala Muralla de la Marina. Here, classic concerts, musical recitals, conferences and presentations of books take place. Several styles of music such as jazz, folklore and folk songs are part of the programme.

Address: Calle Beatas, 15

mimma.es

MIMMA

Museo & Tour Málaga - Club de Fútbol

Over 100 years of passion for football can be experienced while visiting the exclusive areas of the Rosaleda Stadium and the museum with its historical collection of documents and trophies.

Address: Paseo Martiricos / Estadio La Rosaleda / Bus Line 17

malagacf.com/elclub/museo

Museo Alborania - Aula del Mar

The marine museum is located at the port and portrays the history of fishing and sailing as well as the maritime flora and fauna of the island Alborán. Fish tanks, marine creatures, model ships, experiments and a movie underline the importance of the sea and inform visitors about the manners and customs of the sailors. The museum is interactive.

Address: El Palmeral de las Sorpresas, Muelle 2

auladelmar.info

Club de Fútbol

Marine Museum

Museo Automovilístico de Málaga

The Automobile Museum exhibits more than 90 car models in ten thematic areas, as well as original hats from the 1920s to the 1950s by important designers and extravagant pieces of art to illustrate the progress of the 20th century.

Address: Avenida Sor Teresa Prat, 15 / Bus Line 16

museoautomovilmalaga.com

Museo Carmen Thyssen Málaga

Located in the Palacio de Villalón (16th century) the Carmen Thyssen Museum houses 230 pieces of work related to Spanish Art during the 19th century with special focus being paid to Andalusian paintings. Furthermore, special exhibitions are offered.

Address: Calle Compañía, 10

carmenthyssenmalaga.org/es

Automobile Museum

Carmen Thyssen Museum

Museo Catedralicio

The Cathedral Museum houses famous works of artists such as Pedro de Mena and José Ribera in the former chapter house. Further exhibits are relics, silver, ceramics, carvings and embroideries.

Address: Calle Molina Lario, 9

diocesismalaga.es/catedral

Museo de Arte Flamenco Peña Juan Breva

Lovers of flamenco will find a lovely collection of valuable guitars, vinyl records and recordings, wax cylinders, and works of art from the past 200 years in this museum.

Address: Calle Ramón Franquelo, 4

museoflamencojuanbreva.com

Museum of Flamenco Peña Juan Breva

Museo de Artes y Costumbres Populares

The Museum of Arts and Popular Traditions illustrates the daily life and skilled trades in Málaga since the 17th century. Visitors will be able to gain insight into the city's habits and customs.

Address: Pasillo de Santa Isabel, 10

museoartespopulares.com

Museo de la Cofradía del Santo Sepulcro

The Museum of the Brotherhood of the Holy Sepulchre exhibits two thrones carried during the processions. An art gallery houses wall paintings of resident artists (19th century to the present day).

Address: Calle Alcazabilla, 5

hermandadsepulcro.org

Museum of Arts and Popular Traditions

Museo del Patrimonio Municipal

The Municipal Heritage Museum exhibits paintings, sculptures and graphic works from the city's Municipal Heritage, among which are works by Picasso and Carlos Haes. The whole collection comprises 4,000 exhibits.

Address: Paseo de Reding, 1

museodelpatrimoniomunicipal.malaga.eu

Museo del Vidrio y Cristal

In a homely atmosphere, the Glass Museum houses a private collection comprising more than 3,000 exhibits from glass, paintings, furniture and art objects from different historical periods in a building dating from the 18th century. It is only possible to see the exhibition on a guided tour.

Address: Plaza Santisimo Cristo de la Sangre, 2

museovidrioycristalmalaga.com

Municipal Heritage Museum

Museo del Vino

The Wine Museum gives information about the history and origin of wines from the province of Málaga. Visitors have the chance to taste and purchase wine.

Address: Plaza de los Viñeros, 1

museovinomalaga.com

Museo Félix Revello de Toro

The portraitist Félix Revello de Toro is famous for depicting the feminine body with seductive elegance. Canvases, sketches and drawings count among his most important works. In addition, the museum has renovated the workshop-home of Pedro de Mena.

Address: Calle Afligidos, 5

museorevellodetoro.malaga.eu

Museum Félix Revello de Toro

Picasso Museum Málaga   TIP

The Picasso Museum was opened in October 2003. It consists of more than 233 works of Pablo Picasso that can be visited in eleven different halls in the Buenavista Palace.

The paintings, drawings, sculptures, engravings and ceramics by the artist illustrate the phases of his works from 1892 till 1972 and stem from a private collection by Christine and Bernard Ruiz Picasso.

Furthermore, the museum offers temporary exhibitions.

Address: Calle San Agustín, 8

museopicassomalaga.org

Tip: On Sundays during the last two hours, entry is free.

Picasso Museum

The Russian Art Museum

The Russian Art Museum was recently opened in March 2015. It houses 100 works of famous Russian artists and temporary exhibitions.

Address: Avenida Sor Teresa Prat, 15 / Bus Line 16

coleccionmuseoruso.es

Museo Taurino de Málaga

The Museum in honour of the notorious torero Antonio Ordóñez from Ronda gives information about more than 600 years of tauromachy. Not only costumes but also pictures, posters and valuable exhibits related to tauromachy can be seen.

Address: Paseo de Reding, 8

malagaturismo.com

Museo Taurino

Parks and Gardens

Not to be missed

La Concepción Historical-Botanical Gardens

TIP

Bus line 2 from Alameda Principal to the terminal and 15 minutes on foot or by tourist bus stopping at the entrance of the park

By car: A-45 → Exit 140 → MA-431 → Jardín Botánico

Situated in the North of Málaga, the estate La Concepción was owned by Marquis Loring between 1850 and 1990. Amalia Heredia Livermore and Jorge Loring Oyarzábal created a tropical park on an area covering 23 hectares, which was declared a historic-artistic garden in 1943 and is counted amongst the most beautiful gardens in Europe.

The visitor has the opportunity to experience an adventurous trip strolling via obscure channels or broad paths, past a partly rich tropical vegetation, small brooks, waterfalls and ponds towards the historical viewpoint offering panoramic views of the city. Currently, the gardens consist of a collection of 25,000 plants or 2,000 species from across the world, which are displayed under subject areas including "Around the World in 80 Trees".

Furthermore, it is possible to visit a palace and a small museum exhibiting statues and Roman mosaics and presenting an archaeological exhibition.

Address: Camino del Jardín Botánico, 3

Closed on Mondays

laconcepcion.malaga.eu

Montes de Málaga Natural Park

By car: → A-45 → Exit 124 → MA-435 → Diseminado Casa Foresta Torrijos (52 min./42 km)

Five kilometres from the city, this natural park extends over 4,900 hectares to Colmenar. The highest mountain, La Reine, rears up 1,031 metres above sea level. The park offers a wonderful variety of Mediterranean flora and fauna, which can be discovered either by walking or by bicycle on nature trails.

Besides conifers and cork-oaks, olive trees, almond trees and locust trees, bushes and herbs also grow here.

Many different animals, including birds of prey, badgers and chameleons threatened by extinction are settled in the park.

topwalks.net/de/montes_malaga.htm

Montes de Málaga

Natural Area of the Estuary of the Guadalhorce

By bus line 5 dir. Parque Ocio → M. Curros Enríquez → on foot 1,5 km (45 min./6 km)

By car: → Autovía de Acceso al Puerto de Málaga/MA-22

The Estuary of the Guadalhorce is located near the airport on an island measuring 122 hectares that is bounded by both tributaries of the river. The nature reserve houses more than 260 species of birds for being part of the route migratory birds take on their way from Europe to Africa. There are aquatic plants but also poplars, meadows, eucalyptus, tamarisk and palms.

Apart from the Guadiaro, it is the river most abundant in water in the province of Málaga. It rises from the province of Granada and flows into the Mediterranean Sea to the west of Málaga.

andalucia.com/cities/malaga/home.htm

Estuary of the Guadalhorce

Puerta Oscura

This park at the southern slope of the Gibralfaro owes its name to a gate of the former fortification wall.

Address: Jardines de Puerta Oscura, 1

Gardens of Pedro Luis Alonso

Situated on the east side of the city hall, these gardens cover an area of 6,500 square metres. A mixture of Hispanic-Muslim and French features gives the park an interesting flair. Not only Mediterranean orange trees, cypresses and colourful flowerbeds but also 75 varieties of roses can be admired. Moreover, there is an architecturally interesting pond to relax at.

Address: Calle Roma, 1

Gardens of Pedro Luis Alonso

Park of Málaga

The city garden forms a green oasis on approximately 20,000 square metres in the midst of the traffic. It consists of three walkways with a total length of 2,400 metres and numerous statues and sculptures like for example the one by Don Antonio Cánovas.

In the midst of the rich vegetation, tropical and subtropical plants, numerous benches are available. Taking a carriage ride certainly is an adventure.

Every Sunday after twelve noon, the Málaga Municipal Band, one of the oldest groups in Spain, gives a recital in the bandstand, which is very popular with the inhabitants of Málaga.

Address: Paseo del Parque, 1

Taking a carriage ride certainly is an adventure

Historical San Miguel Cemetery   TIP

The Historical San Miguel Cemetery, neoclassical in style, was built in the 19th century according to the plans of the architect Mitjana in the district of Capuchinos and was consecrated in 1810 when the city was occupied by Napoleon's army.

It is considered of the most significant monuments in Spain.

Famous personalities of the bourgeoisie of the 19th century, who were massively involved in the city's progress, rest here in impressive mausoleums.

Address: Plaza Patrocinio, 3

Open every day from 9am to 6pm.

malagaturismo.com

San Miguel Cemetery   *Bridge of the Germans*

English Cemetery

It was forbidden to bury non-Catholic foreigners on the city cemetery until the beginning of the 19th century, which is why the English Cemetery was eventually constructed.

Among others, the German captain of the frigate "Gneisenau", sunk the 16th of December in 1900 off Málaga's coast, is buried here. Numerous inhabitants who came to the sailors' rescue lost their lives. In honour of these heroic deeds, Germany presented Málaga with an iron footbridge that is also known as the Bridge of the Germans (el Puente de los Alemanes).

Address: Avenida de Pries, 1

malagaturismo.com

English Cemetery

The Port of Málaga

▶ **Enjoy sixteen beaches p. 81**

As much as 3,000 years ago, the Phoenicians used the bay as a trading port and founded a settlement. Due to the extensive expansion of the harbour district up to 2011, it eventually became possible to connect the cruise terminals with the historical centre via the Plaza de la Marina and the Paseo del Parque. Nowadays, it is possible to admit four cruise liners at the same time and accomodate around a million cruise visitors every year. Not only deep-sea vessels can be moored in the port but also yachts and sports boats.

The regular route of the ferry towards Melilla as well as the rise of carriage business and shipyard works thanks to the operation of the container terminal contributed to the fact that the Port of Málaga became the second most important one in the whole of Spain.

Wharf One (Muelle Uno) invites visitors to spend their times in boutiques and restaurants on an area of 55,000 square metres while Wharf Two (Muelle Dos, also called El Palmeral de las Sorpresas) acts as the main promenade. On an area of 14,000 square metres, 408 palms and hundreds of bushes and flowers are planted. Here, some cafes and the Maritime Museum can be found.

Moreover, the Palmeral de las Sorpresas is the venue of the annual book fair, which takes place every May.

The Port Work Committee is located at Plaza de la Marina. The noble building was built in the 20th century according to the plans of engineer Manuel González.

The lighthouse "La Farola" was constructed in 1816 according to the plans of engineer Guzman and is located on the promenade of the same name between the port and the Playa de la Malagueta. Since then, it has been restored several times, the last time by engineer Mauro Serret and the House Julius Pitch from Germany sticking to the characteristics of 31 rays the lighthouse radiates.

The tower measures 38 metres in height, the beacon 33 metres and the scale of the light reaches 25 nautical miles.

Address: Muelle de Cánovas s/n

puertomalaga.com/web/guest

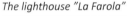

The lighthouse "La Farola"

The Beaches of Málaga   TIP

The 16 beaches of the city, measuring a length of around 14 kilometres, have been certified several times with the Blue Flag for cleanliness and excellent water quality by the European Union. The most important ones to the west of the port are called San Andrés, Misericordia, Guadalhorce and Guadalmar (with a designated area for nudists). To the east lie broad, sandy bays like the Playa de la Malagueta, Baños del Carmen (located on an eucalyptus grove), Playa Pedregalejo / Las Acacias (separated into six small bays by a breakwater) and Playa El Palo.

All of these beaches are within walking distance or can be reached by bus. They are fully accessible and offer parking lots. Almost all of them are connected by a broad seaside promenade. Beach bars and restaurants serve culinary specialities.

View of the bays to El Palo

Trade Fairs and Congress Centre

The Trade Fairs and Congress Centre, as well as the Teatinos Campus and Administration of the University, are located 6km north-west of the port.

The Trade Fairs and Congress Centre, covering an area of 60,000 square metres, was opened in March 2003. The Centre has an exhibition space of 17,000 square metres in two different halls as well as 30,000 square metres outside the building. Furthermore, there are two auditoriums with capacity for 910 and 600 people, two conference rooms for 400 and 375 people and 14 smaller halls. A multi-purpose space of 2,375 square metres can accommodate a banquet with 1,500 guests.

The direct connection to the airport and the technical equipment can accomodate events at national and international levels.

Address: Avenida Ortega y Gasset, 201
fycma.com/en/

Trade Fairs and Congress Centre

University of Málaga

The University of Málaga is a public university with around 40,000 students and 1,300 research assistants. It was founded in 1968 and started to operate in 1972. The University focuses on research on science and medicine.

The Faculty of Science is located on the Campus El Ejido in the city centre while the Faculty of Medicine as well as the Administration operate on the Campus Teatinos in the north-west of the city, realising research projects in cooperation with the Technology Park Andalusia.

Students have the option to choose among official courses of study, preliminary studies in seminars, advanced training courses, sport and cultural activities. Foreign students are offered the opportunity to attend language courses.

Address: Avenida Cervantes, 2
uma.es

Botanical Garden on the Campus Teatinos

Events and Festivals

Where to go

Religious and traditional feasts dominate the lives of the inhabitants of Málaga, which is why nearly every day is characterised by a feast. The new year starts everywhere with fireworks after the inhabitants have eaten twelve grapes, one at each stroke of the bell.

The feast of the Three Wise Men, on the 6th of January, begins the previous evening with a big parade of bands and band wagons throwing sweets into the crowd. It is on this night that the children receive their gifts they yearned for.

Andalusia's National Day dates back to the 28th of February 1980, when the region became independent. It is celebrated as a lively carnival ending Ash Wednesday with the symbolic burial of the sardine.

In these hours, during the early evening, sounds of bands can be heard rehearsing in the city park for the most important religious feast, the Holy Week (Semana Santa).

The traditions of processions date back to the 15th century when the Catholic Church, after having reconquered the city, started to play the Passion of Christ for the Muslim population. As for the organisation, fraternities were founded, to which the penitent (Nazarenos) and the carrier (Costaleros) belong.

42 processions take place during 7 days of ceremony underlying traditional rules, in which 14,000 porters for the thrones are needed.

The summer solstice on the 23rd of June is celebrated at the beach with a campfire and grilled sardines, people burn significantly huge puppets and take a bath in the Mediterranean Sea.

The religious highlight is the world renowned Feria de Málaga in honour of the city's reconquest by the Hispanic Kings in 1487. This giant summer festival usually starts on the third Saturday in August and ends nine days later with huge fireworks.

Many concerts of national pop and rock groups, equestrian events and bullfighting in the bullring La Malagueta are on the agenda. Innumerable marquees invite visitors to dance and celebrate until the morning light and flamenco dancers show their talents on the streets and squares.

Altars in squares and streets on Corpus Christi

In honour of the Patroness Our Lady of Victory, a small Madonna is carried through the streets on the 8th of September.

The Christmas period transforms the city into a sea of four million light bulbs in the form of giant beams of light with festive motifs and bright garlands wrapped around the trees.

The presentation of a crib (Bélen) is part of Málaga's culture and tradition and visitors will find one hundred of them in the city. The biggest crib is located in the city hall with more than 256 figures over 150 square metres.

The Feast of Verdiales is a musical Flamenco competition and is won by the dancer who manages to make his opponent lose his rhythm.

Calle Marqués de Larios during Christmas time

Flamenco in Málaga

The flamenco is rooted in the history of Andalusia as, during the centuries, different groups like the Greeks, the Romans, the Arab or the Roma (also called Gitanos) came to settle here. They left their mark on the music, which did not spread in Andalusia until the 19th century.

Flamenco can be divided into three different elements labelled cante (song), baile (dance) y música (music). The music is accompanied by a catchy beat created by the famous castanets or simple clapping. The flamenco guitar and the cajón, a drum in form of a box, are indispensable instruments. Thanks to fantastic dresses and the "nailed" heels, a flamenco show surely is a unique experience.

flamencotickets.com/malaga-flamenco-shows

Enjoy a flamenco show

Flamenco shows

Kelipe Centro de Arte Flamenco
Calle Alamos, 7 / kelipe.net

Tablao Los Amayas
Calle Beatas, 21
flamencotickets.com / tablao-flamenco-los-amayas-malaga

Museo de Arte Flamenco Peña Juan Breva
Calle Ramón Franquelo, 4 / museoflamencojuanbreva.com

Restaurante Vino Mio   TIP
Plaza Jerónimo Cuervo, 2 / Show: every day at 8pm
restaurantevinomio.com

Theatre

Recinto Eduardo Ocón
Paseo del Parque, 6

Sala Gades
Calle Cerrojo, 5
guiadelocio.com/malaga/teatro-y-danza/malaga/sala-gades

Sala María Cristina
Calle Marqués de Valdecañas, 2

Teatro Alameda
Calle Córdoba, 9 / teatroalameda.com

Teatro Cánovas
Plaza del Ejido, 5 / teatrocanovas.es

Teatro Cervantes
Calle Ramos Marín, 3 / teatrocervantes.es

Teatro Echegaray
Calle Echegaray, 6 / teatroechegaray.es

Teatro Romano
Calle Alcazabilla

Festive calendar of Málaga

Spanish culture in Málaga ensures a great variety of events stretching throughout the whole year. Regular activities are an integral part of the lives of Málaga's inhabitants.

If the public holiday is a Sunday, the following Monday will be a public holiday, too.

January	
01.01. New Years Day / Nuevo Año	Parade of the Three Wise Men
06.01. The Three Wise Men / Día de Reyes	Theatre Festival
	Contemporary Music Season
February	Chamber Music Season
28.02. Andalusian Day / Día de Andalucía	Great Performer Season
	Carnival
March	Flamenco Season
19.03. Day of San José / Día de San José	Málaga Festival - Spanish Film
	Women's Race
April	
Easter Thursday - Jueves Santo	Holy Week /
Easter Friday - Viernes Santo	Semana Santa TIP
May	Book Fair
01.05. Day of the Worker / Día del Trabajo	Sleepless Night / Noche en Blanco
	Organ Music Season

June	The Magical Night of San Juan
	(23.6. / summer solstice)
July **25.07. Day of Apóstol Santiago /** **Día del Apóstol Santiago**	Festival of the Virgin del Carmen Malagueñas Song Contest
August **15.08. Assumption of the Virgin/** **Asunción de la Virgen**	Malaga Fair (9 days) TIP Fishing Smack Regatta Swim across the Port
September **08.09. Day of La Victoria, Patron** **Saint of Málaga / Fiestas** **de la Virgen del Carmen**	Start of the Philharmonic Orchestra Season Festival of the Vírgen de la Victoria World Tourism Day
October **12.10. Hispanic Day /** **Día de la Hispanidad**	October Picasso Events / Octubre Picasiano City of Málaga Urban Race
November **01.11. All saints day /** **Todos los Santos**	International Jazz Festival Fantasy Film Festival
December **06.12. Spanish Constitution Day/** **Día de la Constitución** **08.12. Immaculate Conception /** **Purísima Concepción** **25.12. Christmas Day / Navidad**	Málaga Marathon Christmas Fiestas Verdial Main Festival (28.12.)

Culinary Delights

▶ Where to eat and drink p. 95

As far as culinary delights are concerned, Málaga knows to impress with traditional Andalusian cuisine and it is quite difficult to choose among nearly 700 cafés, bars, bodegas and restaurants because Málaga offers meals for all sorts of individuals, from cheap to luxurious, from a simple bar at the beach to a place of pilgrimage for gourmets.

With the spread of taverns, tapas became popular because it was common to protect drinks in jugs and glasses from dust with a slice of bread, ham or cheese. Tapas simply means lid. It does not matter whether they are taken as a quick snack at the beach, as a varied dinner or as appetisers since these delicious cold and warm specialities exist in innumerable varieties and every bar tends to create its own variety of it.

Meals containing meat are said to be good and solid. The most classical meals are Choto al Ajillo (goat served with garlic) as well as numerous varieties of the famous paella. Málaga is especially famous for pescaíto frito, fried fish, which is prepared in different forms. Nevertheless, the most popular fish are grilled sardines (espeto de sardinas), followed by gilt-head bream and squid (calamar) that are coated with coarse salt, put on simple reed spits and grilled over glowing charcoal in converted fishing boats. Not only visitors, but also inhabitants, know how to enjoy fresh fish in a seaside restaurant in typical Andalusian flair and the Mediterranean Sea right in the background.

Wine from Málaga

Even the Byzantine used to cultivate wine. In the Middle Ages, the fraternity of wine-growers started to supervise the wine-making. Due to a royal decree at the beginning of the 19th century, the marks of origin were introduced to guarantee quality assurance. Two of them are still in use nowadays.

The "Sierras de Málaga" denominate white, red and rosé wines with an alcohol strength less than 15 % ABV while "Málaga" stands for both the sweet, naturally fermented wines (at least 13% ABV) and the fortified wines (from 15% to 22%). To reach the respective alcohol strength, ethyl alcohol is added to the fortified wine.

Furthermore, during the ripening process it is necessary to mix wines from different vintages to achieve the particular taste. In a bodega these wines can be tasted.

Wine from Málaga

Typical Andalusian

Antigua Casa de Guardia

In Málaga's oldest bodega (1840) friendly waiters tap the wine from large barrels and note down the price with chalk on the counter.

Alameda Principal, 18 / good value
antiguacasadeguardia.com

Bodega El Patio   TIP

This restaurant offers 30 different kinds of paella and is a broad pub, which consists of a terrace in pure Andalusian style.

Calle Granada 39
entreplatos.es/wp_elpatio

Bodega El Pimpi   TIP

In the midst of a nice ambience, visitors can drink wine and marvel at signed pictures and messages from celebrities.

Calle Granada 62 + Alcazabilla
elpimpi.com

Café Bar Mercado Atarazanas

Amongst the atmosphere of a central market, visitors have the chance to enjoy fresh fish and seafood, along with some long, cold beverages.

Mercado de Atarazanas
Calle Atarazanas 10
azahar-spain.com/azahartapas/cafe-bar-mercado-atarazanas

Café Central TIP

Málaga's oldest café is famous and well-known for its nine different ways of preparing coffee.

Plaza de la Constitución, 11 / cafecentralmalaga.com

Cervecería Los Gatos

Traditional famous pub offering jamón iberico (Iberian Ham). A free small tapa is served with a beer.

Plaza Uncibay, 9
blog.solaga.co.uk/cerveceria-los-gatos-in-malaga

El Tintero II

It is unusual to order à la carte because guests usually eat whatever the waiter gets out of the kitchen.

Beach of El Palo, Carretera de Almería, 99 / good value
restauranteeltintero.com

La Tetería de San Agustín

In a cosy and quiet atmosphere, tea and cake specialities are offered.

Calle San Agustín, 9 / la-teteria.com

La Tetería de San Agustín

Mañana Cocktail Bar   TIP

This bar is a hub of creativity, culture and fun. It has more than 80 cocktails on the menu, and 30 different beers to choose from. A visit here won't break the bank.

Calle San Juan De Letran, 7 (Plaza de La Merced) / good value
facebook.com/MananaCocktailBarMalaga

Mesón Ibérico

In the artistic district of Soho, this restaurant offers tapas, fish and meat specialities of the highest quality.

Calle San Lorenzo, 27 / mesoniberico.net

Tapeo de Cervantes   TIP

Choose from traditional or more innovative tapas and raciones with delicious combinations and stylish presentation.

Calle Carcer, 8 / info@eltapeodecervantes.com
eltapeodecervantes.com

The Bodegas El Patio and El Pimpi

Activities

Discover all the great things to do

Sightseeing on wheels

Hop-On/Hop-Off bus tour

The red sightseeing buses stop at 14 stations in 30-minute intervals. The traveling time for the entire route is approximately 80 minutes. The closest stop to the Cruise Terminal lies at the lighthouse (Faro Portuario). Audio guides with headphones are available in many languages.

city-ss.es/en

In a horse-drawn carriage on the Ruta Romántica

At the Plaza de la Marina horse-drawn carriages start for a romantic sightseeing cruise to ten hightlights of the city.

guiademalaga.wordpress.com/viajes-virtuales/audio-guias/ruta-romantica

Bicycle tours

On hot summer days exploring the city on a rented bicycle (from € 5) can be refreshing. These tours can be extended to beautiful panoramic rides on the promenade. You might want to book a themed tour.

biketoursmalaga.com/de

Segway Tour

A guided tour on a Segway is still an extraordinary experience, which is bookable for 1 hour leading through the historic city centre or for 2 hours including Gibralfaro.

Address: Calle Trinidad Grund 8 (near Plaza de la Marina)

segwaymalagatours.com

Boat trips

A boat trip guarantees some fresh sea breeze. If you want to take a catamaran to the open sea or a little sightseeing boat trip through the harbor, you can buy tickets for the desired time at the pier on the waterfront. Often, you are already addressed by the crew in passing by. "Birthday kids" go sometimes for free.

Sail&Fun organizes sailing trips in groups lasting several hours. Here you can also hire sailing or motor boats with or without a crew.

Edificio de formación, PPL4, Puerto de Málaga

sailandfun.es

Boat trips start at Muelle Uno

Wellness

Los baños árabes

The Arabian baths are doubtlessly fine remains of the Moorish heritage. Oriental atmosphere with scent of jasmine, different temperatured pools, a steam room, a sauna, massages and hot marble slabs wait here to relax the mind, body and soul. Sweetened mint tea completes a perfect wellness program. An example of Nasrid art is exhibited by the „Hammam Al Andalus" in the heart of the old town, not to be confused with the less recommendable „El Hammam"! Admission at less frequented times is cheaper. A reservation is needed.

Address: Plaza de los Martires 5 / Centro Historico

Reservations by phone: +34 902 333 334/952 215 018

O2 centro

Those who want to indulge in a spontaneous break after the many attractions can visit the O2 Wellness Centre in the El Perchel district. Built in the style of a modern indoor swimming pool it offers various hot tubs, hot baths and a training pool. For regular guests there is a wide range of fitness programs.

Address: Calle Plaza de Toros Vieja, 5

o2centrowellness.com

Nightlife in Málaga

After enjoying a meal in a restaurant and getting in the mood with a glass of sherry, it is common to set off around midnight to go dancing and celebrating.

Popular clubs in the old town are located in the Calle Granada, Calle Beates and the Plaza Uncibay. Younger night owls prefer the district La Malagueta, which distinguishes itself with numerous trendy bars. An excellent nightlife also dominates in Pedregalejo and El Palo, where the language schools of the city are located. Women usually enter for free in most of the discos and bars. There is no particular dress code.

A guided nightlife tour (from € 10) often includes reductions and/or free drinks.

malaga.com/v/nightlife
malaga-university.org/Malaga-Nightlife.htm

Monkey House A discotheque above all popular with Erasmus students, located in the historical town centre.

Calle Álamos, 2 / facebook.com/MONKEYHOUSEMLG

Velvet Club A hip club with gigs and DJ sessions featuring all types of music.

Calle Comedias, 15 / velvetclub.es

Shopping

There are shopping facilities abound in Málaga and anyone, who likes to go shopping and strolling, will be pleased with the wide selection and relatively low prices. Well-known international chainstores like Ikea (Avenida de Velázquez, 389 / ikea.com), Media Markt (the main train station, Explanada de la Estación / mediamarkt.es) or El Corte Ingles (Avenida Andalucia 4-6 / elcorteingles.es) and fashion stores like H&M (Plaza Félix Sáenz, 2 / hm.com), Bershka (Calle Marqués de Larios, 9 / bershka.com) or Deichmann (Puerto de Málaga, Local 51 / deichmann.com) are represented as well as small boutiques and shops, that offer tea, towels or even piercings.

Whether in the beautiful shopping streets Calle Marqués de Larios, Calle Nueva and Muelle Uno or in the many small alleys, opportunity to rest can be

Calle Larios and H&M in the former Félix Sáenz department store

found in numerous cafés and restaurants or on noble marble benches.

Two large shopping centres are located in the city centre:

Larios Centro with around 75 shops

Avenida de la Aurora, 25 / larioscentro.com

Centro Comercial Vialia with 96 stores:

Explanada de la Estación / vialiamalaga.es / tiendas

Markets

Almost every neighborhood has its own market hall and weekly markets. In the city centre this is the Mercado Atarazanas (p. 52). Every Sunday a large flea market takes place on the exhibition grounds (p. 82): Rastro del Cortijo de Torres / mercadillosemanal.com/en.malaga/rastro-de-malaga.

The largest arts and crafts market in town can be visited in the Plaza de la Merced every last Sunday of the month (p. 14).

Arts and crafts market in the Plaza de la Merced

Excursions

Marbella

Daibus main bus station→ Marbella (1 h)
Auto → AP-7 / A-7 → Marbella (63 km) / Parking: Avenida del Mar
andalucia.com/marbella/home.htm

From the main bus station, the exclusive coastal town of Marbella is only 45 kilometres away. Like Málaga, it also has remains of the reign of the Moors. The ruins of a castle and two defensive towers of the Arabic Wall have remained. A town hall from the 16th century and an old church are located in the historical centre.

Visitors pass by numerous craft shops and street cafés in chalk-white alleys. Sculptures by Salvador Dalí are arranged on the boulevard Avenida del Mar. Further monuments worth visiting are the Bonsai Museum, the Museum of Contemporary Spanish Engraving, a fishing port, the luxury marina Puerto Banús and two beautiful beaches.

Route 66 American menu and live music
Antonio Banderas Plaza, Puerto Banús
route66marbella.com

Marbella's yacht harbour

Nerja

ALSA-Bus from Puerto de Málaga → Nerja Cuevas (65 km / 1,5 h)
From Cueva: ALSA-bus dir. Málaga → Nerja (10 min.)
Car → A-7 → Exit 295 → N-340 → Cueva de Nerja → N-340 → Nerja
andalucia.com/nerja/home.htm

A 45-minute-trip by bus eastwards along the coast leads to the small coastal town Nerja, which became famous world-wide for its cave, discovered in 1959. The Cueva de Nerja is 4,823 metres long and is separated into three galleries, of which one quarter can be visited. It is estimated that the caves were populated between 30,000 BC and 1,800 BC.

Furthermore, it is worth seeing the Aqueduct of El Aguila from the 19th century, a baroque chapel (17th century), two churches (both 17th century), the History Museum housing a 8,000-year-old skeleton named Pepita as well as the Balcony of Europe, offering fantastic views of the Mediterranean Sea and the Sierra Almijara.

Teteria Zaidin Cake and pastries well worth the calories
Calle Granada 16 / teteriazaidin.com

Beach of Calahonda in Nerja

El Torcal de Antequera

By car → A-45 → A-7075 → MA-9016 (50 km)
andalucia.com/antequera/torcal/home.htm

The nature reserve Paraje Natural El Torcal de Antequera is located 50 kilometres from Málaga and requires a two-hour-trip by bus or hire car. The nature reserve, around 12 square kilometres in size, with its unusual karst mountains, is located between 1,100 and 1,400 metres above sea level.

Two marked circular walks lead through wildly fissured rocks, gorges and high columns made of stone slabs, which surfaced 200 million years ago due to collision between two tectonic plates. When the weather is fine, the nature reserve offers marvellous views of the coast, the Sierra Nevada and the historical city Antequera. El Torcal counts 700 varieties of plants and 116 species of vertebrates. Furthermore, there is a tourist information centre and a small museum.

Paraje Natural El Torcal de Antequera

Mijas

Suburban train C-1 Fuengirola → Bus M-122 → Mijas Pueblo
Timetable: fuengirola-guide.com/buses.php

By car → AP-7 → Exit 214 → A-387 Mijas Pueblo (Parking: Plaza Virgen de la Peña / Avenida del Compás / 50 min.)
andalucia.com/mijas/home.htm

The town of Mijas, located 428 metres above sea level, in which donkeys are rented for transportation (Burro Taxi), is listed for preservation. The old city centre has kept its Moorish urban structure, and the beautiful park with panoramic views of the Costa del Sol has conserved remains of the former city wall. One of the four chapels named Virgen de la Peña was carved into a rock by the Royal, Celestial and Military Order of Our Lady of Mercy and the Redemption of the Captives in 1548 in honour of the patron saint of the city. In the historical city centre, picturesque alleys run alongside white blocks of houses. It is worth seeing the Miniature Museum exhibiting the painting of Abraham Lincoln on a pinhead, the Bull-fight Museum and the round bullring, which has an outer shape of a square.

Bar El Niño Great food, fantastic staff and good prices
Calle Campos, 26 / mijaslife.com/bar-el-nino.html

Burro Taxi

Ronda

Train (RENFE) from María-Zambrano → Ronda
Car → A-357 → A-367 → Ronda (100 km, Parking near the station)
andalucia.com/ronda/home.htm

This white town has a notable location in the midst of the mountainous region of the Serranía de Ronda 723 metres above sea level. The old town, which is influenced by the Moors, sits enthroned on a precipitous rock plateau and is separated from the modern district El Mercadillo by the 100-metre-deep gorge El Tajo, through which the Río Guadalevín flows. Both districts are connected by three bridges, the most famous of which is the Puente Nuevo constructed in the 18th century. The construction period carried on for more than 40 years. Along with the bullring, it is considered the soul and symbol of the city. It is worth taking a walk through the fir tree forests of the Sierra de Grazalema and the Sierra de las Nieves.

El mesón Rondeño Great range of tapas, good value for money
Calle Pedro Romero, 9 / mesonderonda.com

Puente Nuevo

Granada

TIP

ALSA-bus main bus station→ Granada main bus station (2 h)
Car → A-45 → A-92M → Granada (130 km)
Alhambra tickets: alhambra.info/en

The Alhambra is located in Granada on the hill of Sabikah. The castle complex has a length of 740 metres, a width of 220 metres and consists of several Nasrid palaces. It is recommended that you visit the Generalife Gardens of the summer palace. Visitors have breath-taking views of the city from the terraces of the historical hotel, named Alhambra Palace.

For a walk through the Moorish old town, the Mirador de San Nicolas gives an impression of the enormous dimensions of the Alhambra. For the most part, visitors to the Silk Market above the Square Bib Rambla drink tea in one of the Moroccan tea-rooms and the evening comes to an end in the gipsy neighbourhood Sacromonte with a flamenco show.

Casa Cepillo Cheap day menu (near the Cathedral)
Plaza Pescadería, 18 / granadamap.com/cepillo

Alhambra

Seville

By ALSA-Bus main bus station → Sevilla, Calle Cristo Expiración

By train dir. Sevilla-Santa Justa → Sevilla-San Bernardo
By car → A-45 → A-92 → Sevilla (216 km/Parking Paseo Colón)
sevillaonline.es/english/seville

By bus or train Seville is two and a half hours away from Málaga. The historical city centre is still in very good condition and almost every monument is within walking distance. In 1218, the mosque of the Moors was a consecrated cathedral. The bell tower La Giralda is symbol of the city. The Real Alcázar, a Moorish palace, nowadays still functions as a royal palace and possesses broad gardens from different epochs. The Plaza de España impresses with its bridges, pavilions, galleries of arches, two towers and a fountain with high spouts. It is worth seeing the Plaza de Toros (La Real Maestranza), the University located in the former Royal Tobacco Factory, the city hall, the Casa de Pilatos and the Metropol Parasol.

Bodega Santa Cruz Busy with locals. Food is tasty and homemade
Calle Rodrigo Caro, 1 / facebook.com/BodegaSantaCruzSevilla

Metropol Parasol

Gibraltar *(130 km)*

Daibus → La Linea de la Concepción → Crossing the border on foot (500 metres) → Bus Line 5 → Reclamation Road (takes 2.5 hours to reach the border)

By car → AP-7/A-7 → Exit 119 Direction San Roque / La Linea → Border (Traffic drives on the right in Gibraltar/ Parking according to map/ 1 hour and 40 minutes)

EU nationals need a valid identification card to enter Gibraltar. Upon departure, customs regulations valid in the EU must be followed (ec.europa.eu/taxation_customs/index_en.htm). Day tickets for the use of buses and cable car (including nature reserve) in Gibraltar can be purchased at the Gibraltar kiosk on the Spanish side of the boarder.

The Gib, three square miles in size, as this British crown colony is lovingly called by their citizens, is characterized by religious tolerance and a colorful mixture of cultures and populations. Numerous Christian churches, four synagogues, one Hindu temple and a mosque. The dialect Llanito, a hybrid of English, Spanish and other Southern European languages, is spoken besides English. The British exclave is ruled by a governor while foreign policy and defence are still competences of the British crown. Approximately 30.000 balloons rise into the air on September 10th, the national holiday, one for each and every citizen.

Strategically positioned, *The Gib* has always been a disputed area. Several monuments, cannons and (military) installations illustrate British superiority. It is said that once the last macaque has disappeared, the British will lose this important fortress. As their population on the **Upper Rock** is continuously increasing, however, this event is unlikely to happen any time soon. Alighting from bus line 5 at Reclamation Road, the **Hindu Temple** located at Engineer Lane which can house up to 600 visitors will be the first point of interest. The **Grand Synagogue** dating from 1724, the oldest synagogue on the Iberian Peninsula, is located next to the Temple.

Engineer Lane / gibraltarhindutemple.org

47/49 Engineer Lane / jewishgibraltar.com

From Bell Lane, turn left into **Main Street**, a **shopping mall** for duty-free products, to find numerous traditional restaurants and pubs in British style offering Fish n' Chips along with a perfect draught pint. You will also come across the **Cathedral of St. Mary the Crowned** which was constructed on the foundations of the former main mosque using previous elements like the Moorish courtyard.

215 Main Street

Typical pub on Main Street

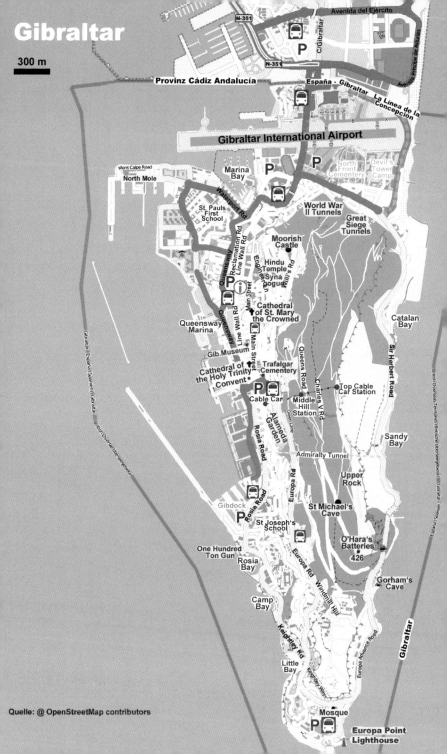

Just a few steps away, the **National Museum** of Gibraltar offers a panorama of more than 20,000 years of cultural and natural history. One of these rooms is dedicated to **The Rock** exhibiting an accurate scale model of the rock more than 8 metres length. A well-preserved Moorish bathhouse dating from the Marinid dynasty gives an impression of Islamic culture during the 14th century and an accessible cave once inhabited by Neanderthals illustrates natural history. Furthermore, **Gorham's Cave** 40 metres in length and located on the Eastern part of the rock can be visited.

18/20 Bomb House Lane / gibmuseum.gi

The **Cathedral of the Holy Trinity**, an Anglican church from the 19th century, especially known for using Moorish elements such as horseshoe arches is located here.

Cathedral Square - Main Street / holytrinitygibraltar.com

Portal of the convent *Garrison church King's Chapel*

Changing of the guard of soldiers of the Royal Gibraltar Regiment takes place regularly at the main entrance of the **Franciscan Convent** which has served as the official residence of the governor of Gibraltar since 1728. Meanwhile, the adjoining **King's chapel** serves as a garrison church to British military personnel where two British governors are laid to rest.

290 Main Street / convent.gi

Located in the South is the small **Trafalgar Cemetery**. The name is misleading due to the fact that victims of three epidemics and seamen who died in sea battles are buried there. While seamen who died as a consequence of the Trafalgar Battle were buried at sea, Lord Nelson was buried in London.

Trafalgar Road / visitgibraltar.gi/trafalgar-cemetery

The **Botanical Garden Alameda** directly adjoins the Valley Station of the **Cable Car**. Amongst wild olive trees, cacti and a Dracaena several monuments, busts and weapons illustrate the important military history of Gibraltar. The open-air theatre is used for open-air events.

Red Sands Road / Bus 2, 3, 4, 9 / gibraltargardens.gi

To understand the military history, it is recommended to visit the **100 Ton Gun** that could reach the entire bay of Algeciras due to its angle of 150°. **Pasons Lodge fortress** located on the hill of **Rosia Bay** serves as a training ground to the military. Currently, it is not possible to visit the fortress.

Rosia Bay / Bus 3, 4, 9

Europa Point with its red-white lighthouse offers an impressive panoramic view although the southern-most point of Europe is located in Tarifa and the biblical mountain Jebel in Morocco can only be seen in clear weather. During the summer, visitors who wish to bathe at **Sandy Bay** can take a free shuttle bus from the free parking lot.

Located in a small pilgrimage chapel, the **Shrine of our Lady of Europe** impresses with its two-metre-high wood carving portraying the image of our Lady of Europe. The Saudi king Fahd presented the Muslim population with the **Ibrahim-al-Ibrahim mosque** which is among the biggest mosques located in a non-Islamic country. The interior is luxurious. The minaret measuring 232 feet in height is crowned with a brass half-moon measuring 19 feet. The mosque can be seen from miles away when illuminated.

Europa Point / Bus 2
trinityhouse.co.uk/lighthouses
visitgibraltar.gi/mosque

Lighthouse at Europa Point in Gibraltar

The Upper Rock Tour

The Rock of Gibraltar, home to numerous Barbary macaques with its panoramic views is Gibraltar's main attraction. Entering the **nature reserve** is fairly expensive, although visiting several monuments is included in the entrance fee. Experienced drivers may explore the Rock by car arriving at each attraction by travelling on narrow streets. The number of parking facilities is limited. It is easier to explore the area by taking the cable car that carries the visitor to its terminus at 412 metres in only six minutes. Hikers will find well marked trails.

Saint Michael's Cave, the biggest of the 140 caves in the rock, is located in the south 800 metres downhill. The stalactite cavern served as a hospital during World War II and is nowadays used as a concert hall due to its fantastic acoustics. The Lower St. Michael's Cave impresses with a cathedral-like atmosphere and a 40 metre long crystalclear lake. The lower cave can be visited on a guided tour that has to be booked three days in advance.

visitgibraltar.gi/tour-lower-st-michaels-cave

900 metres further downhill, heading north, the **Apes' Den** can be found at the middle station of the cable car. Since the day the Barbary macaques became bored with their rock and started to conquer parts of the city to the annoyance of local residents, they are being observed by the Gibraltar Ornithological and Natural History Society (GONHS). All 230 maca-

119

ques are registered via a microchip, are provided with water and feed every day, given regular veterinary examinations and are subject to birth control as their habitat is limited.

gonhs.org

From this point it is 1.5 kilometre (approx. one mile) walk towards the Northern series of underground tunnels and three more sights. Alternatively, visitors can take the **cable car** bound for the foot of the hill at middle station and the bus line 1 direction Willi's Road at Market Place.

The 200-year-old **Great Siege Tunnels** impressively illustrate the defence system during the Great Siege at the end of the 18th century. Peering through the cannon holes, one sees the isthmus and neighbouring Spain, looks across the airport runway which is the only runway crossing a four-lane street in the world. Furthermore, it is worth having a look at the **graffiti** scratched into the rock by soldiers.

Barbary macaques are not easily agitated

The World War II tunnels with their artillery positions dating from World War II are part of the 53 kilometres (32 miles) long tunnel system. Underneath these tunnels, there is a Moorish castle with its landmark **Tower of Homage**, a tower reconstructed during the 14th century.

Mediterranean Steps

Adventure seekers can climb the spectacular path running at the east side of the Rock along the cliffs. Its steep steps carved in limestone start at a height of 180 metres at the Southern entry of the nature reserve. The climb is 1.4 kilometres long (approx. one mile) and ends at the **O'Hara Battery** on a height of 419 metres next to the peak.

Information Centre

Tourist Information Office
13 John Mackintosh Square

Internet
gibtours.com

gibraltar.com/sightseeing

Cable car/nature reserve tickets:
gibraltarinfo.gi/product/cable-car-copy

Bus timetable:
www.gibraltarbus.com/gibraltar-bus-timetables-2016

Useful information

Money
The currency of Gibraltar is the Gibraltar pound. Pound Stering is also accepted (at the ratio of 1 to 1).

Post Office/ Telephone

The Royal Gibraltar Post Office provides special stamps which are popular with tourists and philatelists due to their limited availability. The Main Post Office is located in 104 Main Street.

Telephone: the country calling code is 00350

Restaurants

Verdi Verdi Affordable café offering delicious cakes as well as fresh and kosher main dishes (fish but no meat)

2A Main Street / verdiverdi.com

Gatsby's Delicious snacks and international food

1 - 3 Watergardens 1, Waterport Road / gatsbys.gi

Jumpers Wheel Famous fish restaurant offering a wide range of fresh fish

20 Rosia Road / t1p.de/facebook-Jumpers-Wheel

Unterkunft

The Rock Hotel**** Luxury historic hotel, overlooking the Gibraltar Botanic Gardens

3 Europa Road / rockhotelgibraltar.com

The Rock

Worth Knowing

Accommodation

From luxurious to simple and cheap, there are hotels and pensions in Málaga for every occasion and demand.

Vincci Selección Posada del Patio *****
Luxurious design hotel in a central location with authentic gastronomic offerings and private parking spaces.

Pasillo de Santa Isabel, 7 / vinccihoteles.com

AC Hotel Málaga Palacio ****
Centrally located hotel with excellent service, comfortable rooms, spa area and sufficient parking facilities.

Cortina del Muelle, 1
ac-hotel-malaga-palacio.hotelspainmalaga.net/en

Hotel Molina Lario ****
Modern and comfortable hotel with spacious rooms and abundant breakfast buffet.

Calle Molina Lario, 20-22 / hotelmolinalario.com

Hotel Parador de Malaga Gibralfaro ****
Spa hotel in exposed location with views of the city, free parking facilities and an excellent value for money.

Castillo de Gibralfaro /
parador.es/es/parador-de-malaga-gibralfaro

Hotel Don Curro ***
Popular middle-class hotel in a prime location with parking garage, spacious rooms and rich breakfast buffet.

Calle Sancha de Lara, 7 / hoteldoncurro.com

Hotel Itaca Málaga ***
Modern, comfortable hotel in the heart of the historical centre.

Calle Compañía / itacamalaga.com

Hotel Carlos V **
Centrally located hotel with great value for money.

Calle Cister, 10 / hotel-carlosvmalaga.com

Hostel Casa Al Sur **

Popular, cheap and child-friendly pension in a prime location.

Calle Molinillo del Aceite, 5 / hostelworld.com

Hostel Feel Málaga *
Cheap pension in the artists' district of Soho, assuring friendly service.

Calle Vendeja, 25 / feelhostels.com

Terrace of the Hotel Parador   *The Hotel AC Palace*

Information

Pan-European emergency number: 112
Ambulance Service: 061
Police: 092 / 091
Fire Service: 080
Airport of Málaga: 952 048 484
Central Station María Zambrano: 902 240 202
Central Bus Station: 952 350 061
Port Authority: 952 125 000
Port Terminal: 952 125 026
Málaga Council: 010 or 952 135 000

British Consulate
Edificio Eurocom
Calle Mauricio Moro Pareto, 2, 29006 Malaga

Tourist Information Municipal Office
(Oficina Municipal de Turismo)
Plaza de la Marina, 11

Internet
info@malagaturismo.com
malagaturismo.com
puertomalaga.com
theTravellers Video Guide: bit.ly/malaga-video-top12

Public Transport

Trains
Railway station: Explanada de la Estación
AVE: High-speed trains connect the provincial capitals
RENFE: Local trains

interrail.eu/trains-europe/high-speed-trains/ave
renfe.com/EN/viajeros/horarios.html

Suburban trains leave from Centro-Alameda
C 1: Málaga - Airport - Fuengirola
C 2: Málaga - Álora

Calle José M García Caparrós
renfe.com/viajeros/cercanias/planos/malaga.html

Metro
The Málaga Metro started to operate in July 2014. Further stations are still under construction. Currently two lines are operating:

Line 1: Atarazanas - Universidad - Andalucía Tech
Line 2: Atarazanas - Palacio de los Deportes
Timtable: metromalaga.es

Bus
Central bus station: *Paseo de los Tilos*
Main bus station (harbour): *Av. Manuel Agustín Heredia*
Timtable ALSA: alsa.es

The buses by the Empresa Malagueña de Transportes (EMT) leave the bus terminal Alameda Principal and operate daily between 6.45am and 11pm, leaving every 10 minutes. Between 11pm and 6.45am, some night buses operate every 30 or 60 minutes. It is recommended to buy a ten-journey ticket (Tarjeta EMT) at a tobacconist's since this ticket is not only more practical but also cheaper than buying a single ticket for every journey.

Timetable: emtmalaga.es

Sightseeing Tour
The red sightseeing buses operate between 9.15am and 7pm every 30 minutes (Duration: approx. 80 minutes).

city-ss.es/en

Taxi
Taxi rides are generally cheap. The price depends on the day of the week and the time of the day. For baggage passengers have to pay an extra fee.

Register

129

130

132

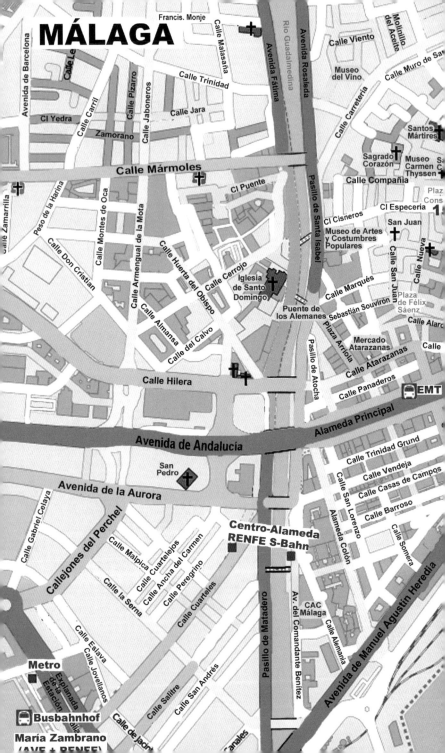